Sex And Death: and other Metapoems about Religion, the Stars, and Hating your Parents

Z3nith Finnell

BookLeaf Publishing

India | USA | UK

Sex And Death: and other Metapoems about
Religion, the Stars, and Hating your Parents
© 2023 Z3nith Finnell

Presentation by *BookLeaf Publishing*

Web: www.bookleafpub.com

E-mail: info@bookleafpub.com

ISBN: 9789358736632

First edition 2023

A Poem

I was once speaking with Poe,
He spoke great wisdom to my poetry;
Said "Every poem should be a crow:
A reminder that you'll die,"

But that's rather a grim quote,
Yet that's not the only tip I received;
Once, to me, a friend wrote,
That every poem should tell a story;

But my teacher also disagreed,
Saying there are only so many stories to tell;
The same seven poems, no one would read,
So I had to invite my own idea;

I thought: We all live a story,
And we all are going to die;
So like that, we are poetry;
I grew nearer to the truth;

Every poem has a different feeling,
Whether they are happy, sad, sane,
Or leaving us mad and reeling,
Poems experience all human emotion;

For that is all poems really are,
A depiction of men and their character;
Varyingly dark, unique, or bizarre;
Every poem is human,
And humanity is poetry;

The Cosmos is Inside Me

The Cosmos is inside me;
But one will not find in I,
The potential, magic, or beauty,
That exist in the sky;

I mean that inside me,
There is a mystery;
Not in the realm of biology,
But a void in Identity;

From myself, I am so far,
As one is to another star;
The unknowns of deep space,
Are reflected in my mirrored face;

Recently, I was made happy,
Twas the last time you called me She;
You threw me over the moon;
Twas enough to make me swoon;

But we've not visited the moon in so long;
So maybe I heard you wrong;
A when I thought you said Her,
I misheard a rocketing slur;

Inside me is the cosmos,
It has nothing to do with you.
But it would alleviate all my woes,
If you took in the view;

If you have the ability,
Bare witness to me!
I wish for you to see,
And love me indiscriminately!

I wish to show the true me!
You could set me free!
Then I will abolish the mystery,
And explore the cosmos inside me;

Beautiful Fields

I walked through the beautiful fields,
The beautiful fields of beautiful women,
And the beautifully ladies painted the fields,
The beautiful fields of beautiful crimson;

In the fields, I saw no green blades;
I only stepped over the beautiful ladies,
All of them thrown on a beautiful blades,
And painting red the wonderful daisies;

And I step around their bodies,
Prodding with my ugly feet,
I taint their beautiful bodies,
Beautiful bodies void of heat;

Oh, how I wish I looked like them;
How I wish I were in these fields forever,
But only if i was beautiful like them,
Then we could lie together;

If only I was not so ugly,
But filled with beauty and perfection,
As they would not accept someone so ugly;
These muses have never faced rejection;

Looking over the horizon, I am alone,
Despite surrounded by beautiful cadavers;
With each other, they're never alone;
How I wish I could lie under their banners;

Then I traveled around the beautiful fields;
On one hill I found a clean sword,
Just one of many that polluted these fields;
It was a source of beauty I could afford;

I could finally be beautiful like them;
I could explore the beauty under my feet;
I would always be among beauty like them;
So easily, I could purge my ugly heat;

Finally I could become beautiful,
And after I throw myself on this steel,
I would join them and be beautiful,
And forever live in this beautiful field;

And If my flesh is visited by any women,
Only for a moment will I be puzzling;
I will lead the way to lying like these women,
I will be a beacon with potential dazzling;

To lie in this field is to be beautiful,
And if I, with my ugly feet, can do it,
I am proof that anyone can be this beautiful;
Only the worst sin of all one must commit;

Reminiscing on a Date with God

We used to love this cafe;
How often we'd meet here for dinner;
But to see you now, I must pray,
Pray you'd dine with this sinner;

As I sit here, with my cup of cheap tea,
You are relaxing upon a cloud;
As you taught me, I'm dipping my biscuit,
And scaring the staff with weeping aloud;

Oh, would you ever come see me?
For I can't see you beyond the shroud;
Oh, how I'd pay to have you visit,
But is leaving heaven even allowed?

If you have wings, you could retreat,
To your new friends of heavenly light;
Or perhaps these friends I could meet,
And show them our favorite places at night!

The waiter asked if you are running late,
I had to tell him we had our last date;
I don't know but why he looked quite sad,
If you are at peace, that is reason to be glad;

Though I can't imagine the stress you're under,
To be ruler of the kingdom above Earth,
With infinite devils waiting for your blunder,
And always having to appear full of mirth;

Though I'm sure it's a task you take in stride,
For before you were holy, you were still great,
Full of ability and well deserved pride;
I would be first to live in a world you create;

I think on you and time's passage escapes me,
My tea's gone cold, but I am already content;
It's the one ability I think I have over thee,
As your hungry and resolve were never bent;

Like all the Gods before and still true to you,
You are a great mystery to me,
Something beautiful I wish to pursue,
But now, you are even more mighty;

I hate that now I'm not your only devotee,
And I hate that they don't understand you;
Too often with them, I disagree,
As they could never know you like I do;

Perhaps I'll simply bite my tongue,
I know in time, you'll tell them what for,
And tell your story I know to be unsung,
But for now, their assumptions I'll ignore;

The waiter now has brought the check,
And again, I've been made a crying wretch;
It begins to rain as my tears hit the deck;
Do you cry with me? Or is that the stretch?

They say you care for all your creations,
Or even as God, does love bore you?
What now are your justifications,
To act like those before you?

I am aware, that it is unfair,
To wish you with me and not up there;
But I confess you to be my only friend,
One I will miss until I see you at the end;

How Useless is the Poet

How useless is the poet,
One who adds no work to society,
But rather writes hate on it,
While acting with highest righteous piety;

How unlikable is the poet,
One who never experiences love,
But always falling into it,
And escaping it like a dove;

How fleeting is the poet,
Always acting as a shut in,
Sinking into a void-like pit,
With dust growing on their skin;

How depressing is the poet,
Always lost in their work,
Never stepping outside of it,
And with the pen, going berserk;

How mad is a poet,
To think they can write on the world,
Though they know nothing of it,
As they never leave the ball they've curled;

How stupid is the poet,
To write poetry on love,
Having never tasted it,
That love they've only read of;

The Cycle

One big bang marks the universe's start,
And it's wonderful and full of art,
And It's only us and there is nothing else.
Only we are allowed to experience this;

But soon, infinity is rather small,
And the days go by with a crawl,
We've soon enjoyed and mastered all the arts,
And sampled the love in our hearts,

And this begins the big crunch,
To my heart, space delivers a punch,
As the world caves in, and devores us,
All our love, our art, is reduced to dust,

But this being packed so tight,
Some sort of bang it ignites;
And the universe is created again,
And again it is filled with content,

Seeing you again in the stars is a feeling sublime
It's like experiencing this love for the first time;
And again there is much love to make,
And again, before long, it all feels fake,

Then it repeats, over and over,
There is a crunch, and love is over,
But this nothingness always leads to a bang,
After which the bells in my heart again sang,

But our love burns out after not too long;
Maybe together this universe doesn't belong;
Yet with the nothing comes loneliness,
In the crunch, I experience unique lowliness,

But you come running back to me,
Do you again want to try infinity?
I was starting to believe you only liked the bang,
And was willfully ignorant of that Yin's Yang;

A Short Game

I give Death a most harrowing leer;
But he alone is not the cause of my fear,

It is instead the game at hand,
One with consequences most severe,
All depending on the face the coin will land.
That will determine if my story ends here;

From his game, I must not turn tail,
Or He will ferry me to the land of the dead;

At least this way, I could yet prevail,
But equally likely: He takes my head,

Time seems still and my face goes pale,
I feel the fate's hands tightening my thread;

The coin falls in His hand, boney and frail,
"Call it," and His words bring me dread,

To Death I answer, "Tails!"
He then reveals the coin: misread

God's Greatest Gambit

I am not a man with my mind gone mad,
No, in this moment, I am liberated!
And I am flying,
Flying higher than I have ever flied,

No, in fact, I am a god,
Gods know I play chess with the others,
Not that I play chess like a god,
For God is the grand master,

And every move of mine is a blunder,
And every move, I offer material,
Material the greedy father in the sky takes,
And he takes, and he takes, and he takes,
And then he's moved five times,
And I have lost on time,

And God pierces my mind with an army,
And the army moves diagonally,
Past my stone walls guarded by rocks,
From which I throw an armada of rooks!

And I refuse to be called a mad man,
For only a sane man would pick a fight with
God,
And an even saner man would call herself God!
For God I am, but I do not play chess like one,

Yes, One, there are many,
And I am all of them,
All of the god's worst parts,
I am God, and I am gods,
I am a pantheon,
A pantheon of madness,
But I am not mad,
For I write poetry,

And as God cares not for His creations,
So too does this aggregate god cares not for her
line structure,

But it's all methodically planned and plotted,
I assure you, it's all in my plan,
For God cares not enough to rhyme!

So a Good Captain I'll Be

A good captain, goes down with her ship,
And a good captain I wish to be;
Yet here I am, still floating,
Adding weight to the debris;

With no crew to lead and nothing left to do,
I find myself studying the water below;
Cutting the silence, I ask myself dumb
questions,
"Why is it so hard to let go?"

Suddenly, I am saved,
As if God had given me the object of sung
prayers;
Right past the wood, and under my hand,
Floats an unopened case of flares;

I try not to look at it;
This is my great opportune moment;
They'll be songs written of my adventures!
So I let the flares go without movement;

A good captain, goes down with her ship,
So a good captain I'll be, at the bottom of this
pit;
All the good captains I hear talk of on shore,
Are all those captains that will never again see
it;

Sex and Death

This poem is about sex and death,
But then so is all of poetry;
It's all emotion, promises, and last breaths,
Something to experience in both sex and death;

A poem is the match that starts fires of passion,
And a poem is exhaustedly asking "what's left,"
When all the art and bedsheets are ashen,
Is the anxiety in my heart the agent of Death?

For you, I dressed nice and nicely undressed,
For you, I shaved and put makeup on my breast;
With the rhythm of poetry, my love is expressed,
And one more night, our issues remain
unaddressed;

And when we die and my funeral you attend,
Will you only be a fan of my promiscuous
works,
Or confess to the world to be a long lost good
friend,
One who knew personally my personality
quirks?

Poetry describes living, and in poems I write my life,
But in my fictitious biography, sex and death are rife;
For I was only a lonely poet, one that never had a wife,
And one whose only friend in bed was the knife.

For Your Own Good

You can't understand, but you are wrong,
Please leave me now, for who you love is sick;
It is contagious and will catch you before long,
My most deadly world view, most pessimistic;

You may love me, but I will show you hate,
For hate is all I see in the world and in your
face;
Now you say you love me, but I know our fate,
After a month, it is discontent you'll embrace;

For hours now, you kiss me without end,
And now we both laugh, love, and smile;
But soon we will know that we both pretend,
And being together will tire you before a while;

This will be due to no problem in our
relationship,
But simply to the magical sight I will give you;
I will gift you eyes that see only issue and
hardship;
At first you'll hate it, but that hate will hone
your view;

All of our walks in the park shall inspire
anguish,
For as we walk, I will point to all the vultures'
feasts;
Soon, your observations of beauty I shall
vanquish,
With help of litter rife, couples unhappy, and
birds deceased;

Gems and reason to smile in this world are rare;
While things to hate are always common and in
plain view;
I will change you to notice only that with a
bedeviling flair,
As it is my obligation to help you see the world
more true;

Now you are naive and blind to the world's
nature,
Yes, you enjoy the birds and their silly songs,
But than that simple happiness, the world is
greater;
You seem to need my help in seeing Her wrongs;

But if you are not ready to shed your naivete,
I will not force my superior sight upon you;
You need only drop your love for me and go
away;
For if you pursue me, your worldview i promise
to undo;

You Know I Love You

I love you, you know that right?
Though I never wish to see you,
And all your words I choose to fight,
I love you, through and through;

I show you love only how my mother loved me,
Forget for a moment all the times I curse her,
And forget also how my mother I never see,
She taught me through her love how to endure;

It pains me that you think I hate you,
When I am only a practitioner of tough love;
Those many times from the nest, you I threw,
I only wished to teach you flight, my dove;

I admit I am not the best mother,
But I am also the only one who'll love you,
No where in the world will you find another,
Go, try and replace me, I will be here until you
do;

The Purple Flower

The world is many things,
But mostly, It is cruel;
Especially in this land without kings,
Where the air is always terribly cool;

Boring through the ice never gets easy,
And every inch I carve feels like the first;
I can only form holes through which I squeeze,
Until of course my pickaxe led the ice to burst;

I was let into an igloo made for ancient man;
All the walls glistened blue with specs most
star-like;
This was nature's beauty, crafted before art
began,
And the statues of this gallery stand on
stalagmites;

But one beauty far surpassed the rest,
Shining its radiant light through halls of cold;
At end of this cave, I'll find the end to my quest,
A shining purple flower, with six leaves of gold;

This was my greatest discovery,
But journals will only write of the trip;
Of the purple flower, they'll write a brief
summary,
And right over it, readers will skip;

The Trick of Perspective

For ever step I take,
The wooden floor would quake;
It's a trick to fill me with pride;
So as I walk around the lake,
I feel I control the tide!
This is the trick of perspective;

The sky is beautiful at night,
And the moon is so quiet;
It's a trick to make it seem tiny;
So under the stars I might,
Cover the heavens with my pinky!
This is the trick of perspective;

The insects will climb on my hands,
And I will look down on their dance;
It's a trick to make me feel huge;
So I can laugh at the ants,
When they are killed by a deluge!
This is the trick of perspective;

But the rains still control me,
Able to fill me with melancholy;
It's a trick of nature's power;
So I am still at Her mercy,
And from Him I still cower!
Another trick of perspective;

And nature is quick to correct,
And force from me my respect;
Now I'm on knees and begging forgiveness;
I must remember I am always incorrect,
For nature is the greatest witness!
As only She has the correct perspective;

"I am sorry, I cry, "my pride is a curse!
I am ultimately small in the universe!
I was under a trick!
The only law is yours!
How could I be so thick!
It was a trick of perspective!"

As the Stars Rain Down

You look at me, on this low hill we share,
As the stars rain down upon us,
The air is polluted with heat and despair,
And there are things neither of us wish to
discuss,

You look at me, but you are not crying,
You look fulfilled in a morbid way,
You always told me we were dying,
But now it's real, you were right, today's the
day,

Today is the day the apocalypse happens,
You've told me about this on our first date,
We are kissed now only by the stars and ashes,
You seem ready, you've accepted our fate,

You begin to recite me lame poems,
But you are too cynical to deliver them right,
You recite the arts as if they were omens,
And no emotion in either of us do they excite,

"Ashes to ashes, dust to dust,"
Why must you be miserable at this moment?
Why can't you focus on us, for just once?
Why now do you only focus on atonement?

I look at you, but I am not crying,
And I'm not smiling, as the stars rain down,
I am only dancing, spinning, and flying,
I ask you to join, but you continue to frown;

I want you to kiss me,
Maybe then we'll be alright,
But you are too lost in your words of misery,
To realize this to be our last night,

Why must you be so stupid?
In this last moment, take my hand,
But in your lap, your hands are rooted,
Thus historians will not see you as my man,

May the scholars see me as you do,
Oblivious, crazy, and a dancing fool,
But I just want to enjoy the view,
The stars are falling, and it's beautiful

Him

Yes, I cried when I heard, of course I did;
We'd go to church together and pray,
And he felt like a part of me;
But I am confident in saying he's dead,
Because that part of me I can feel decay;
Meaning that myself I can now wholly be;

My relationship with him was most intimate,
We would go everywhere together as one,
He was more confident and prettier and spoke
for me,
But our relationship was also most intricate,
He was favored by our mother and everyone,
He outshined me in every way, and I hated him;

And no, I'd never kill him!
And no, I didn't help him disappear;
Why can't you just accept you overlooked me,
Until the spotlight on him went dim;
Do you only now realize I'm here?
Or are you only now unable to ignore me?

I've been here the whole time,
In the shadow of the boy you loved,
Just behind all of his impressive passion;
But now you treat my existence as a crime;
All because to the side I refuse to be shoved,
And you lack any real love or compassion;

You make me wish I could disappear,
And rematerialize somewhere kind,
Somewhere he had never been;
And in your life I'd no longer interfere,
And soon after, I'd be out of your mind;
And a new life I could begin,
One free from the expectations to be him;

What Did I Do

The one day I forget my umbrella,
It rains, and it rained rather hard;
All I held was my novella,
Which, now wet, I must discard;

But that's life;

I was bit by a snake yesterday,
And with venom, my leg did ballon;
Now my favorite game, I can't play,
As my skill were crippled by the wound;

But that's life;

A made a friend this week,
She's beautiful, funny, and taught me how to
sway;
But on where she lives, we didn't speak,
And now, forever, she's gone away;

But that's life,
And I know not what I did to deserve this;

Then, all at once, the rain clears up,
And you are visiting me in the hospital;
Beeps fill the room as faster you make my heart
pump,
You're here, and I didn't expect you at all;

I already wrote a stanza on you,
I was much sadder then;
Again, you are a most sublime view,
One that makes me instantly zen;

After hours, you have to leave again,
But that's life;
We'll meet again, though I know not when,
And I know not what I did to deserve this;

A Poet's Dream World

The poet's head slips between her hands,
Slamming into the dreamworld's sands;
The creative awakes to a land of queer
formation,
Surrounding her is an infinite source of
inspiration;

Swimming in the air, now painted with hues
indescribable,
Are strange creatures of parody and senseless
biology;
This is a land morbidly beautiful and unstable,
Rapidly changing and plagued with the demons
of psychology;

Looking to grab the poet, from the sand
monstrous hands burst;
She screams and the vibrations she birthed
become alive;
The living air manifest as a feathered beast,
fights the first,
And follows the colorful thing under the sand
again with a dive;

Far off, atop a mountain of fire stained like
glasses,
Sits a castle constructed of light and held
together with purple tacks;
With an impossible and ridiculous step, the
sands the poet surpasses,
Landing her inside the fort without need of
attacks;

On an hourglass shaped thrown sat an infinitely
long haired white being,
Six golden wings flapping on its bareback,
creating the air's special flavor;
The white fleshed being speaks to the poet,
"Like what you are seeing?"
And its knowledge of vernacular particularly
stuck out and scared her;

"You seem to forget," the white humanoid said,
"That a land of dreams-"
The wings on its back stopped flapping and
moved again in reverse,
"Is also-" and the rest of the sentence was
drowned out with screams,
As from the wings, dark hues and deathly smells
dispersed.

Grays, blacks, and unbearable heats seized the
desert of dreamland,
As its sparing and playful creatures begin melt
and disappear;
The poet is attacked by whispering hateful
voices they cannot understand,
Besides their ridicule, no inspiration may be
found here;

The poet's head hits her desk,
She awakes to a vision of blur;
She remembers nothing of dreamland but the
grotesque,
For nightmares were always more poignant and
real to her;

Does Jesus Hate his Dad?

Does the half human Jesus hate his dad?
Or in the father does he see no bad?
For even though He is the reason we live,
He doesn't seem at all supportive;

For God is a most absent father,
Though, this leads Him to be no bother,
For God left his son solely with the mother,
And didn't care who he left to suffer;

For when Jesus traveled the arid desert,
And was being stoned in the city's streets,
Never was there God, even as a peasant,
Never was there God, to clean his son's feet;

You may call to Him in a moment of need,
"Forgive them father, for they know not what
they do!"
But as His son was hung up to bleed,
Was God even present to take in the view?

I never met my father until after death,
Not because he died while I drew breath,
But because he was God, and I mortal,
And my life, unimportant to Him, was dull,

So until I walk along the clouds with Jesus,
I shall cross these burning sands alone;
But when I greet my father, like Oedipus,
I shall introduce my only tutor, the stone;

I Remember the Stars

Oh I forgot to tell you,
I saw the stars last night;
They reminded me of you,
So beautiful and bright;

I remember how you loved the stars,
And how every night you'd lay in our small
lawn,
And you'd search the sky above that house of
ours,
Only to see that all the star were gone;

I remember how I'd hold you in our bed,
And how every night you cried,
For you missed the stars like you miss an old
friend;
I'm only sorry that this is the time they don't
hide;

I like to think the stars were coming to see you,
But they were too late to make the wake;
So they stayed to do the best they could do,
And join me, and in my suffering partake;

Even though they were before beautiful to us,

Seeing the stars last night brought me no joy;
To arrive so late, it felt almost malicious,
Like with my heart they meant to toy;

But I don't want to sully the stars for you;
They truthfully were as wonderful as I
remember;
I only wish I could discuss them with you;

Goodbye

If a tree falls when no one is near,
Does it cry or roar for only dear to hear?
And is the dear conscious enough to fear?
Or to God is the creature not so near?

If a God makes a world, infinite and pretty,
And fills it with no sentience or sapience,
Would the world even exist to pity?
Or was its whole creation extraneous?

If an author writes pages of poetry,
And the art is lost and never tasted,
Even if it were infinitely pretty,
Then was all the writer's time wasted?

If a reader starts a poem or story,
And the read is never completed,
So they never experience its glory,
Then should it have ever been-

www.ingramcontent.com/pod-product-compliance
Lightning Source LLC
La Vergne TN
LVHW010916200726
843509LV00013B/1965